Even Birds Leave the World

Selected Poems of Ji-woo Hwang

EVEN BIRDS
LEAVE THE WORLD

SELECTED POEMS OF JI-WOO HWANG

Translated by
Won-Chung Kim
and Christopher Merrill

Korean Voices Series, Volume 10

White Pine Press • Buffalo, New York

White Pine Press
P.O. Box 236, Buffalo, New York 14201
www.whitepine.org

Acknowledgements:
The translators are grateful to the editors of *Circumference: Poetry in Translation,* where several of
these poems first appeared, and to Shari DeGraw, who printed a broadside of "Sitting Cross-
legged and Thinking about the World Outside."

Cover photograph: Cranes Flying Above Korea's Demilitarized Zone.
Copyright ©2005 by Hyunsook Sohn.

First Edition

Publication of this book was made possible with public funds from
the New York State Council on the Arts, a State Agency,
and the National Endowment for the Arts,
which believes that a great nation deserves great art,
and by generous grants from the
Korea Literature Translation Institute
and the Sunshik Min Endowment for the Advancement of Korean Literature
at the Korea Institute, Harvard University.

Printed and bound in the United States of America.

10-digit ISBN 1-893996-45-X
13-digit ISBN 978-1-893996-48-8

Library of Congress Control Number: 2005905698

Contents

Part III

PREFACE

Four white-necked cranes flying in a grey sky. What's missing from the photograph on the cover of Ji-woo Hwang's *Even Birds Leave the World* is the background: the rice paddies of the Demilitarized Zone between North and South Korea—an ecological haven, which is also one of the most dangerous spots on earth; the thud of shellfire from artillery practice; the crackle of the propaganda broadcast over loudspeakers on both sides of the barbed wire fence running the length of the peninsula; the occasional explosion set off by a deer stepping on a landmine, though local lore has it that animals can sense where the mines are laid; and the whir of the cranes' wings, which inspired the poet-photographer who took this photograph to write: "where peace lies underground, like mines..." Ji-woo Hwang's poetry works in a similar fashion: the surface is all light and movement, but danger lurks in the depths, in the inner recesses of meaning. His work is beautiful—and terrifying.

Which may help to explain Hwang's popularity in South Korea, where he has received most of the major literary prizes and his books sell tens of thousands of copies. His imprisonment during the military dictatorship earned him the affection of his countrymen. And his poems continue to find readers in his newly democratic land, for they mix lyrical intensity with an acute political sensibility, creating an uneasy tension that makes them by turns moving, humorous, and unnerving. Nor is he afraid to offend, speaking truth to power, whether his subject is the oppressiveness of dictatorship or the emptiness of consumerism. If poetry, as Octavio Paz suggests, is the freest activity of the spirit, then Hwang's verses are emblems of liberation. Like the birds invoked in the title poem, which "separate this world from theirs/ and fly away to some place beyond this world," his work soars from the here and now to the eternal.

His exploration of the intimate connection between the sacred and the profane, the political and the quotidian, and the logical and the surreal, is the key to understanding his poetry. Line by line, he veers from one realm to another, reminding us that a poem is a magnetic field which attracts disparate elements; that the route to the invisible is always through the visible; that mystery inheres in the world; and that even if our experience is nameable its meaning is ultimately unknowable. A short prose poem heaves the point:

LIKE DEW ON THE GRASS

Oh, the sound of water dreaming of reincarnation, yearning to be born again; and the lachrymal gland of the grass eavesdropping on the sound; what is alive only lives by calling its name while it lives; what is isn't what it should be, nor is this life. I wonder how calm it will be inside that blazing flame! Holding a bruised candle, I'd like to enter the dew and fall asleep.

Few can sleep for long in Seoul, where the poet teaches drama at the Korean Academy of Theater, partly because it is a bustling capital of seventeen million people, and partly because of the uneasy truce between North and South Korea: the unspoken fear back of every transaction on the Korean Peninsula—social and political, cultural and spiritual. Hwang was born during the war, in 1952, and his poems describe a life governed by the inescapable reality that all hell can break loose at any time. "You have to live, don't you?" he remarks in a poem to Charlie Chaplin. "Therefore please survive by any means." The poems of Ji-woo Hwang help us to do just that.

—Christopher Merrill

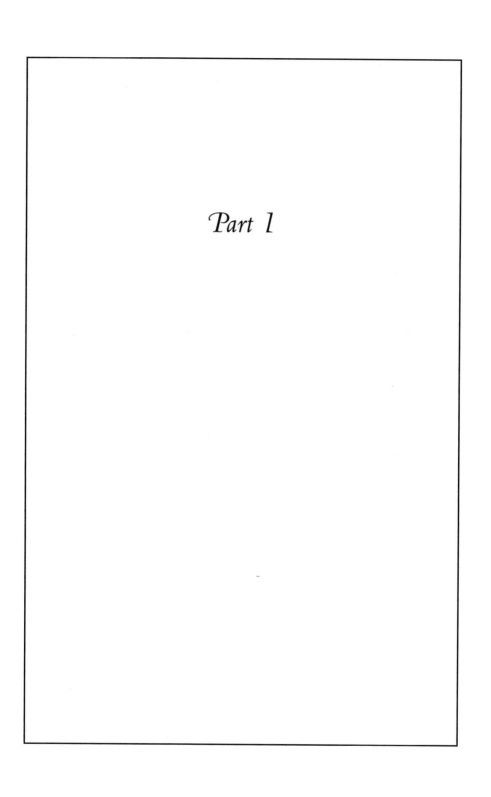

Part 1

Even Birds Leave the World

Before the movie starts
we stand up and listen to the national anthem.
Forming groups on Eulsuk Island,
on three thousand miles of beautiful land,
the flocks of white birds,
honking and giggling among themselves,
take flight from a field of reeds.
They separate this world from theirs
and fly away to some place beyond this world
in single, double, and triple file.
I wish we could giggle among ourselves, and behave outrageously,
and form our own lines to file out in.
We'd like to separate our world from this world
and carry it on our backs
and fly away to some place beyond this world.
But when we hear "Keep the Korean people safe forever!"*
we all collapse
into our chairs.

* The last phrase of the Korean national anthem.

For the Unanswered Days (2)

Whatever the season, these were the condemned days,
days without festivals or wreaths,
mad days when the baptism of blindness ran wild—

By the forsythia blossoms, we were
doused; by the azalea blossoms
we were tear gassed. We lost
our nationality, we went color blind to ideology.
Behind the dense fog and suffocating royal azaleas
we turned into paranoid babblers.
And we were paranoid, we were lying flunkies who coughed and coughed.
Dangerous ideologues who could neither raise our hands
nor even let out a cry.
Restless skeptics who watched "in slow motion"
the pictures of us carried away in bundles.
These were the comatose days.

History

On December 29th, my mother threw steamed rice cakes into the sea in front of our house and smoothed its scattered waves. The next day a cold rain poured onto the laver field. We just looked into the eaves of the rainy spell: poverty was our custom. My heart at high tide worked harder, my cotton clothes carried the stench of my family's wet flesh. Hearing the current swiftly ebbing from the front yard, we remained at the lower shore.

The unnamed islands moved far from view, and the wooden boats that left late sailed back and forth between them. Instead of entering the sea, I listened to the sound of waves breaking over the jar stand in the back yard. In the empty jars the cries of the birds of Sol Island, from which my father left, never stopped. When I could no longer hear which valley deepened across the water, the receding southern bays cried bitterly.

My mother wouldn't let me go outside, and in the courtyard the smoke fluttered again. The myopic winter sea was thinning at the sparkling edge of my eyes. When my father was dragged from the house, the waves at the ferry were as calm as this. If I stood by the shore, flocks of exhausted water birds would be shoved into my dizzy knees. To me, they looked like white funeral flowers flown in from some remote island. The corollas of the flowers were so bright I wished I could fall asleep. In a flash I saw my father coming and going in my mother's dream of conception, and I crossed the oyster flats and hurled nets into the phosphorescent night sea. The flowers decorating my father's bier were endlessly crossing the early morning sea.

The wind that blows every two weeks raged. But the wind had no sound of the wind, like my body after death; the wooden ships returned empty. To avoid the smell of the seaweed, the birds flew from my knees to the interior. The people near shore followed the white cloth of their headbands and moved inland, while the women bowed two and three times for their reincarnation, throwing steamed rice cakes into the laver field in the rainy season. I dived into the heart of the writhing sea and pulled out all the ailing seaweed living on the bottom.

A country collapsed in the courtyard, and cabbages floated on the dense sea. I wonder who will haul up the phosphorescent jar from the womb into which I cast my net.

Like Dew on the Grass

Oh, the sound of water dreaming of reincarnation, yearning to be born again; and the lachrymal gland of the grass eavesdropping on the sound; what's alive lives only by calling its name while it lives; what is isn't what it should be, nor is this life. I wonder how calm it will be inside that blazing flame! Holding a bruised candle, I'd like to enter the dew and fall asleep.

Bird Returning to Its Nest (2)

The bird flew into the deep cochlea where he could barely hear his own song, which marked the circumference of the forest. The bird built his nest in the woods and cried several octaves above hearing until he lost his voice... doubting... in between... whether there was another forest beyond the one in which he had built his nest.

The Day I Entered the Castle

No, it's you out there, outside the door, who must be consoled. I've seen the handles clinging to you. For the unanswered days hanging from the handles, I allow myself to enter the most solitary land on earth. I give up my future. In a note written in red, "Summer, 1984."

Daily Spot Inspection

Yesterday I returned from driving a stake into my ears.
Today I put up a barbed wire fence and bandaged my eyes.
Tomorrow I'll shovel dirt into my mouth
and stuff it with cotton.

Day by day,
night by night,
I bury parts of myself
as the evidence of my life
and to survive.

To Detective Kim Who Is Humane, Too Humane

Detective Kim and I can talk frankly now. My wife also finds "something humane" in him—he buys toys for our children, she serves him coffee—though at first she was wary of him. He even bows to my old mother. Probably because of his humanity, we seldom discuss politics. But once I praised Bulam Choi's performance in *The First Republic.*

Performance? Are we not also performing roles, Sir? He seems happy to be called "Sir." Because he laughs so hard, I laugh with him and answer his question about how I'm doing. He wonders how I can live on so little. I answer him. He asks about my health. I answer him. He tells me his own history, though I have never asked about it.

He descends from landlords in the Hwanghae province of North Korea. In his youth he saw family members taken away by men from the Ministry of Home Affairs, he knows how terrible man can be. He crossed the 38th parallel, led a harsh life, enlisted in the marines, dedicated himself to his profession. He told me why people loathe him when he visits their homes. He laughs a lot; he has good manners; sometimes he even seems to have compassion for things. I told him he's always welcome. He invited me to enjoy a cup of Soju with him someday, though he also lives on a meager salary. After he left, I stopped mulling over our "performances."

The Agony Column

Jongsoo Kim: Disappeared May 1980
No word since. 3rd draft notice to report by Nov. 3 delivered.
Please come home. – Sister.
If you have any information, please call 829-1551.

Kwangphil Lee: Kwangphil, no explanation necessary.
Just come home and we'll talk it over.
Mom is in critical condition.

Soonhae Cho: 21 yrs old. Father is waiting.
Come home soon.
It's all my fault.

Crouching,
I move my bowels.

A Firebird Shooting Sparks

In that flame I cried and asked them
to spare my life,
to forgive me just this once
because I wanted to live; in that flame
I couldn't kill myself but cried instead.

What I couldn't endure,
what I couldn't bend my knees for,
these things
I acknowledged.
I fluttered my wings.

While my wings fluttered in the underworld,
I heard someone
calling my name and I
promised I
would yield.

Falling into the ashes
I wished I had never been born
again in the flesh
and that I would never be born again
as a shattered pot.

Folding my wings, I
laid my head
before the early morning sea,
the morning country over which I'd like to fly,
toward the high window a few hours before sunrise.

A Long Corridor in the Lock

The sound of footsteps and people coming
along the long corridor within the lock—
I'm scared of them.

Mountains of water flow through the nostrils
of the lock; the sound of water,
pond skaters, and water grass
floating in my meninges
circle around my auricles two or three times
and suddenly stop to exclaim,
"Speak out!"

In the gullet of the lock
a telephone rings again, burning me.
My throat takes
the cold hilt of the sword;
And when I'm stabbed
I answer them:
"Let's renounce our humanity!"

When the acoustic wind blows through the hole of the lock,
zelkova leaves quiver. Someone grabs my throat
and shakes me. Two-sided papers flutter
from every bough, and the last leaf
steals my fingerprint.
I'd like to fall asleep. I wonder
"Why do I have a body?"

The sound of the door closing from outside,
footfalls, and people leaving
through the long corridor in the lock.
Collapsing, I ask forgiveness
and finally say to the fly,
THE ONLY WAY TO FLY.*

*A '60s Hippie motto

Beirut, Beirut!

The morning papers say, *Bloody Cry* and *An Exile of Sorrow*, and in the evening, *We'll Never Surrender.*
The headlines in the morning and evening papers are full of variety:

Singing My Country, They Pledged to Fight
When the PLO Leaves, We'll Return to Our Land
Scattered Sparks, Never Extinguished
Every Road Leads to Jerusalem
Photos of Arafat at Every Muzzle
Vowing to Fight Underground Throughout the World

(Ah, what a relief: it's all foreign news!)

And the photos (sent on the 21st from Beirut through AP-Yonhab):
1) A hairy middle-aged man in military uniform says goodbye to his daughter.
2) A boy soldier with an MI6 and a graying man with an AK47 are heading for Beirut in a Lebanese Army truck.
3) A Palestinian woman kisses Arafat on his forehead, as if she were his mother, and he lays his head on her breast. The caption below the photo: *Goodbye, Arafat.*
4) This is real art, a scoop: a soldier's wife, open-mouthed, face distorted, holds a rifle overhead with both hands. (She looks like she's in childbirth or being raped.) The morning paper calls it *The Writhing of Deep Sorrow*, the evening paper, *The Wriggling Farewell.* You, ignorant Israeli soldiers, give me back my son and husband! You, bastard sons of Abraham, Moses, David, and Solomon, you should be hacked to pieces.

The Wailing Wall seems deaf to the wailing outside the wall. I wonder whether this foreign news transmits sorrow or not.

Before the West Wind

That silver aspen, whose dry boughs take the wind into its body and mind, looks like a martyr suffering persecution. But on second glance it looks like a martyr who wishes to be persecuted.

The Wooden Pony and My Daughter

The market's on the way home, and if you follow the lane for a hundred meters you'll find Honam Butcher's. If you take the lane by the fish shop on the right, you'll come to Silim Bath, a public bath. Behind the bath is an empty lot on which stand the salt shop and the tile factory. The salt shop is a wooden shack with a slate roof. Take the narrow path through the tenement houses. The eighth house, the half-slated one, is mine. I live in this house, translating books, writing articles, sometimes writing poetry. If my wife grows anxious, I take my five-year-old daughter to the empty lot and play with her. In the shadow of the tall sycamore old people play cards.

Some days an old man enters the shade, pulling a cart on which stand six wooden ponies. For 100 won a child can ride for 20 or 30 minutes. I put my excited daughter on the white pony, pulling its ear to rock it up and down. Ah, my pretty daughter looks as if she could break the springs of its four legs and fly into the sky before my eyes. Letting its mane wave in the wind, she seems to have entered into the sandy wind coming from the tile factory, into Noryung, the land in the Maritime Province of Siberia, or even into a distant invisible land.

My Wife's Handicraft

Even early in the morning my wife
beats the children with the palm of her hand.
For the 200 won
it costs to buy "Banana Kick" or "B29,"
they cry bitterly, revealing their
red uvulae. It's not just for the damn TV.
She says she has to cure them of their bad habits,
but she is, in fact, playing her hand
against my silence and inability, my overconfidence—
the fact that her husband's home during the day.
Her silent charge kills me
whenever she opens the door
to the meter reader and the salesman.
With my alibi I steal away
from the house where my wife gives
piano lessons to neighborhood kids,
and on the hill from which
I can look down upon the packed city streets
and the new houses built deep in the mountain range,
I exile myself.

In the Lowlands of Silim

Unemployed, prowling the marketplace,
I realize I'm still far from hitting the "real" bottom,
still very far from it.
I sigh,
I confess the bottom looks far away.
But what's far away can be seen. The very things under my feet,
spread over unfurled plastic sheets:
pickpurses, sowthistles, mugworts, wild leafmustards, elm bark;
then anchovies, brown seaweed, sea lettuces, green seaweed,
dried laver fronds, and baby pollacks;
and sitting next to them on the sheets,
opening mussels with a stainless knife,
or short-necked clams,
or peeling potatoes and soaking them in water,
the strange, cold bottom
crushed under my feet,
oh, my mother!

Trace III—1980 (5.18 x 5.27cm)
   by Lee, Youngho

That road is straight
as if to say time can be represented by space.
The road is covered with black asphalt
as if to say it's a desolate midnight when even the street broadcast is over.
A yellow line is drawn down the middle of the road to indicate the
         diaphragm of a life
as if it were the very bottom of First Avenue blacked out by a deadly
         silence,
on which people whose minds are dead but whose bodies are still alive
lie flat and listen to the footsteps,
or as if it were the bottomless pit of my fever and cry.
A white X is drawn
on the white ↓ beside the yellow line,
and the street light is shattered into pieces on the cross.
From the street light to the white X, or
beyond the white X, or
over the rim of the canvas to the white wall,
traces of army boots hurrying by are imprinted,
like tens, hundreds, and thousands of seals.
As if to say it's the last road
on which you will never return.

Looking for a Way to Live

I go out. Come back. Sleep. Get up.
Shit. Brush my teeth. Wash my face. Today, just the same. I go out
as usual, the strangest person in the fifth republic.
I walk. Read everything
in the street. Safety first.
Our capital. Our technology. Our subway. The fourth stage
of the construction by Hanshin Co. The construction site of Kugje Group's
    headquarters.
Pusan New York Bakery.
Ground Floor: coffee house by day, beer hall at night. 1st Floor: Samsung
    Electronics Agent. 2nd Floor: English and Japanese Academy. 3rd
    Floor: Jinwoo Lee Dermatology Clinic. 4th Floor: Sunmin Jungang
    Church, Presbyterian Church of Korea. 5th Floor: Aerobic Dance
    and Health Club. Rooftop: Advertising tower with signs for miracle
    drugs for pregnancy, hemorrhoids, and venereal disease pasted on
    electrical poles.
No gap. But if you push through
the billboard with gaps
and watch out for strangers and call the police if
suspicious...   Seated on the overpass all day long
displaying combs, nail clippers, belts, ear wax removers, handkerchiefs,
        and coin purses
an old woman's life on 2000 or 3000 won a day
I have crossed
holding 20,000 won worth of goods
she is chased by the police ah, this life! ah, this overpass!
ah ah ah ah the backbone of this life quivers
ah ah ah ah ah the legs of this life tremble
on the street the future isn't seen
the future is seen too clearly
not knowing anything   babbling
tattling, whispering, breathing heavily, panting
The streets are full of sexual desire   like a boil before it festers   a wealthy

                muscle
a tower crane   hauls a steel beam 100 meters into the sky
ah ah ah ah ah ah ah I watch the audacity, the diligence and insanity
the sincerity and blindness   I watch and watch
a jackhammer ferociously pounds holes into the asphalt
in the pebbles, in the rocks
                an excavator relentlessly digs up layers of sediment but
the fact that the excavator unexpectedly digging up pure, white, fine soil
                is 20 meters underground
                is not a passion or a credo   but compassion
                as a person who knows it, I
I must restrain myself from seeing the world with the eyes of compassion,
as a person who knows it, I   but
ah ah ah ah ah ah ah, what a pity! a young man
who broke into the bank with a homemade bomb blew himself up (Sept 2,
                Jungang Ilbo)
a naked hostess from the bar was strangled by her secret lover (June 15,
                Hankook Ilbo)
a night guard turned into a burglar at midnight (Dec 12, Kyunghyang Newspaper)
a son hammered his drunken father to death (April 11, Seoul Newspaper)
a policeman raided a gambling den and stole the stakes (July 26, MBC Radio)
a teacher molested a girl student (Nov 30, Chosun Ilbo)
head priests brandished swords and clubs at Shinheung Temple (August 3,
                KBS Radio II)
a group of adolescents burned to death at a discotheque (April 14, Yonhab
                News)
an ex-deputy chief of Korean CIA swindled 1 billion won (March 6,
                Donga Ilbo)
ah, time passes well
the blind days pass well
the days on which I didn't even lift a finger pass well
the days on which nothing happens—no accidents, events, affairs,
                happenings, auto-happenings, and mishaps even those days
pass well

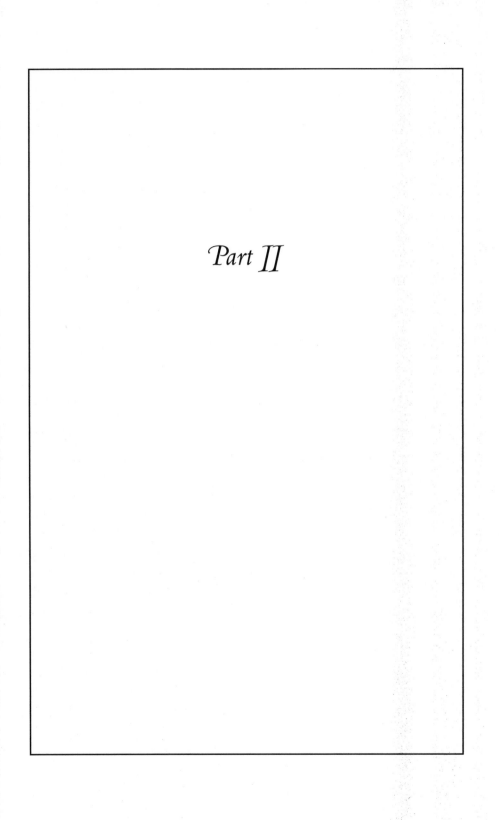

Part II

From Winter Tree to Spring Tree

A tree becomes a tree
from its own body.
With its whole body a tree becomes a tree.
Sinking its whole naked trunk into the earth
at -13°C and -20°C
and raising its head,
the tree stands naked and helpless.
Raising its two hands, as if to be punished,
the tree lifts its body and long suffering life.
"It can't be like this." "It shouldn't be like this."
Though its whole body burns with anger and frustration
the tree resists and endures, and then pushes its body
from below zero to above zero, to 5° and 13°C.
The tree pushes itself so blindly
its whole body is bruised
and crushed.
While its body is broken apart
it pushes out new sprouts with its hot tongue
which will grow green leaves slowly, gradually, suddenly.
Striking its body into April's blue skies
the tree becomes a tree from its whole body.
Ah, at last,
the blossoming tree is a blossoming tree
from nothing but its own body.

Today, Flying Over the Sea of Proverbs

The bird beats itself to fly away. Beating itself to fly over the waters of its life, the bird travels to the other shore, connected to this sea—far away, unseen, though it surely exists.

Variety Show, 1984

That damn guy must want to die. You bastard, are you blind? What did you say, you bastard? How dare you call me a bastard. In the left turn lane, a taxi-driver and a chauffeur (ah, he owns a Mark V GLX Ford) scream at each other, pointing at the sky.

The church steeple seems to lower the sky. A red neon cross flashes above the red neon sign, "Youngdong Cabaret." The transmission tower of a wire service company...I wonder what damn souls it communicates to in the wee hours of the night.

I can't believe it. I'll never enter their "Promised Land." Invaders!

You should sing a song, *kungjajak jakjak.* If you don't, you'll be penalized, *kungjajak jakjak.* Fifteen brass coins.

My writings-actions are not answers, but questions, questions, ephemeral, without substance, endless doubts and questions...
Endlessdoubtsandquestions?

We congratulate you on your endless doubts and questions (satirically), at the twelfth Evergreen Literature Award ceremony. It was strange. She thought they didn't mean it. Although she received bouquets and had her picture taken with prominent writers and an interview with the press, she felt so empty that on her way home she was in a frenzy, as if she'd been raped.

Miss Lee undressed herself and dove under the sheets.

And then the morning sunlight through a crack in the blinds. Bright dust. Despair, despair so severe I wanted to die or kill someone.

When I got on the bus this morning, I saw vomit on the second seat from the back, on the right. People competed for the seat, but then ran away in terror. The vomit consisted of 55% rice grain, 15% *kimchi,* 10% bean sprouts, 7% crushed tofu, 5% white and yolk of a fried egg, 5% hot pepper powder, and 3% other stuffs.

God of Heaven and Earth, these are the foods of our world. Shovel them into our bellies. Feed us generously.

Minister of Agriculture and Fisheries, come forward to answer some questions. Why the hell doesn't the government raise the price of rice? Congressman K from the Kukmin Party, who no longer has any face to lose, pounds the table, raising his voice, but farming villages are passé.

My God, how can she just leave it there? A gentleman in his forties in the second seat from the back, on the left, raises his voice hysterically. Instead of answering him, the woman conductor covers the seat with a newspaper and returns to her place.

Four Seoul National University Students Arrested at Demonstration: On the 15th Kwanag Police in Seoul arrested four Seoul National University students, Youngsu Kim (22, mathematics major) Heja Lee (21, biology major), Huiyoung Hue (23, journalism major) and Yunho Shin (22, geography major) for violating the law on assembly and demonstration. They are suspected of leading the demonstration and handing out a thousand pieces of anti-government printed materials called "Democratic Students' Declaration for Resistance" at the student's cafeteria and library around 1:40 on the 11th of the month.

Father, Mother, I'm terribly sorry. I pounded nails into your hearts.
See! Do you remember what I told you.
The Attorney General said this huge financial scandal has nothing to do with high government officials, but I wonder if the newspaper, which doesn't know how to use a question mark—"this huge financial scandal has nothing to do with high government officials?"—is really a newspaper. Is it a newspaper or an official gazette?

Why do they talk so much, the damn bastards! Torture them! Beat them to a pulp!
Hahahahahahahahahahahahahahahahahahahahahahahahaha
He laughs without moving a muscle in his face, iron-masked man, brazen face.
Did you hear that a forty-something movie director got an eighth-grade girl pregnant—how did he do *that?* How is it possible?
Every reality is hell. Every single one.
Especially in the context of the history of fighting colonialism and imperialism, the phenomenon of single-party dictatorship, which was common

among newly independent third-world countries, can be justified, cannot be, can be, cannot be, no cannot be, yes can be...

Yesterday, on a panel sponsored by the Academy of Korean Studies, five professors from the national universities spoke.

In the window of the psychiatric unit at the university hospital red geraniums bloom and wither feebly (F.O.). In a flower, however insignificant, there must be something like a spirit or a soul. In the red geranium there must be the spirit or the soul of a red geranium.

You say a spirit? What's the use of a damn spirit, a good-for-nothing spirit?

Nosuk Park, 23, lathe man, monthly salary: 100,000 won. With his oily hands he eats sweet potato tempura. The black dirt under his fingernails disgusts Sunyoung Lee (21, a junior studying nutrition at Ehwa Woman's University), who is watching him. Waiting for the waitress to serve him new tempura, Nosuk Park chews slowly, looking askance at the girl who looks like a college student. Sunyoung Lee is really offended. Under his malicious gaze, eager to swallow her, she feels as if every nook and corner of her body has been laid bare.

Twenty years from now, I wonder if his son will meet her daughter like this.

Both sides of the supermarket wall are covered with mirrors. One mirror watches another mirror, and the mirror watches the mirror that watches the mirror, and the mirror watches the mirror that watches the mirror that watches the mirror...

Head Priest Imjae got down from the preacher's desk. In one hand he held his meditation cushion, in the other Priest Magok. He asked him, "Where did the twelve-sided Buddhist Goddess of Mercy go?" When Priest Magok tried to sit on the woven chair, Imjae picked up his staff and smashed him. Priest Magok grabbed the other end of the staff and that was the posture in which they entered their quarters.

An automaton in a human shape swings a red flashlight at the entrance to the subway construction site. Endlessly the light swings even after 11 p.m. UNDER CONSTRUCTION. BEWARE OF FALLING! UNDERGROUND 20M

Take everyone and everything underground to prepare for that day!

Well, this is pure speculation, but what would you do if, and only if, atomic bombs were dropped from the sky over Seoul as soon as I finished talking?

I'd follow the CBR rules, as I learned in reserve forces training.

I'd sit quietly.

I'd pray.

I'd shave while my heart said, "Even if the world were to end tomorrow, I'd plant an apple tree today."

I'd change my underwear.

I'd bow to my parents.

I'd hug my kids.

I'd drink rare whiskies I had hidden for myself.

I'd make love with my wife one last time.

Then do you know that atomic bombs are already loaded in the sky above?

Ten million beetles steadily suck sores day and night, though they know and don't know it, and can't speak about it even though they know it. Blind life in a flame, day and night. Miserable, miserable, ah, miserable.

If we all die at the same time, there will be no death for us.

A young mendicant monk scowls at the three-month-old baby on the back of a woman in her twenties. A man's larva, which bloomed in splendor, a lotus from the loins of lust! The baby looks around, stripping the eyes of the world (January 1, 1984. In the line of people returning from Kangnam Terminal. Waiting for the bus to Chonju).

But this lust is what supports mankind.

At Jongro 3 ga. On a billboard of the Piccadilly Theatre is a painting of a famous actress with her legs spread. For three months straight. In the lower right-hand corner she embraces a naked man, arching her back. Breathless, with her mouth wide open and eyes closed. When the life and culture of an age turn pornographic, I wonder what's the use of writing poems, lying on the cold floor at dawn. What a funny thing to do.

A kerosene heater in the health club set fire to the hotel. At the windows of the seventh and eighth floors, a man and a woman, unknown to each other, struggle to catch the lifeline dropped from the helicopter. Some fail to hold the line and fall to their deaths, with onlookers watching. On the ninth and tenth floors many people are burned to death.

Hey, this can't be the first time you've seen death? Yes, it's only thirty dead.

But over a drink Wonwu Kim, a novelist, said the Korean middle class will never want the two Koreas to be united.

The separated family, after a brief meeting, separates again.

The past is regrettable! The past is sad! The past sad! The past! Sad! Sad indeed! Enough to make me grind my teeth.

The boy who was killed for shouting "I hate communists" now stands as a statue in a quiet elementary school yard.

At rush hour, county workers, bank tellers, and village officers stand at the crossroads, wearing a signboard, "Follow the Street Rule," or holding pickets.

The end of the rule is stretched along the blade of a sword.

Endless marching in the name of progress.

Elementary schoolchildren stop reckless drivers with their yellow flags.

All stopped. In every office, at every school and private or public work place. Because at exactly five o'clock the national flag-lowering ceremony begins, all passersby stop and bow to the invisible flag. Energetic high school students salute.

Observing this, BIG BROTHER from 1984 says, "It's good to see."

The Constellation of My Mind's Map

Dawn arrives only for the one who stayed up all night.
Camel,
watch the dawning horizon
with your sand-stuck eyes.
Pushed by the wind, a new day arrives.
So let's get up again and start.
The desert growls again in my stomach.
Presently I have neither sword nor scripture.
Scripture doesn't teach the way.
The way
is behind the mask.
Following the steps from which no one will be excused
you and I are walking toward the distant blue sky.
I am you,
so we are ourselves.
The constellation of our minds' map
has led us this far.

Bird Leaving Home

The bird
doesn't leave a trace;
only its weight on the bough on which it perched
sways for a while.
It
doesn't cast a shadow
on its perch.
Even in the air
there's no trace of its body passing through.
Probably because it has no past,
it has no body odor,
no stench.
It has no tears to shed,
but it knows how to fly into a squall
with its poor, fragile, naked body.
With its dreamy, longing eyes
it can see through the wild winds into the next life
and find there the forest of tomorrow.

Sandpaper

This desk at which I'm taking a break
was once a forest in Borneo.
Adding fat to the belly of the ancient rings,
the raw timber happily fed on the wind off the Indian Ocean.
With a day's wage in hand, Mr. Mahatra, a lumber jack,
swallowed his bitter saliva, and went home.
At Daesung Lumber in Inchun,
Sukman Kim, a novice factory worker,
sandpapered it all day long. Endless work, like a desert.
Miss Lee, who receives 13,000 won a month for cleaning and accounting,
put lots of papers on the desk to be signed.
Is my labor an act of prostitution?
I hear cries from every direction.
Give me my share,
my share.
This desk at which I'm taking a break is,
so to speak, my disguise.*

* Korean college students, concealing their education, used to work in firms as laborers to
incite unrest among the other workers.

Trees Are Hard

Trees are hard.
Hard and dull.
The dark bark has the sulky look of protest
against something unpleasant.
Trees, growing long faces in every season... reconciliation is what's needed.
Trees are rough. Firm.
Depressed. Unrestrained.
Because they're famished,
they suck in air, dirt, noise, and odors
until their bellies are about to burst.
Their burning desire makes them green and greener.
The color green is the lust of the trees.
For a while, trees recover their minds.

Sol Island

I spend the night at the Wayfarer's House on my way to Oran.

"Where are you from?" asks a nameless woman.

"You look suspicious."

"Are you from the North?"

She flinches.

"Then where are *you* from?"

She wandered from Yeosu to Youngdeungpo, Miari, Pusan, Mogpo, Wando, and finally to Haenam. After two years in a lodge near Daeheung Temple, she drifted into the marketplace.

"You've finally hit bottom?"

"Your eyes resemble my lover's."

"What does he do for a living?"

"A monk."

He used to pour *Makkoli* for her late at night, then climb up to his hermitage. That monk went to Tongdo Temple, when the mountain bulged with the lust of autumn colors.

She saw him off at Kwangju Terminal.

Then she returned to the sad autumn mountain.

"I myself am a monk returning to the secular world."

She smiles bitterly and crawls into my breast.

I bury this small old ugly woman in my big heart.

"Where are you heading?"

"Oran."

"Can you be more specific?"

"Sol Island."

"Anyone living there?"

"No one."

The hen climbs into her nest and soon falls asleep.

On December 24, 1983, I coaxed a woman to sleep in this world. When I woke at the sound of the bells in the Catholic church announcing the first mass, she was gone. Snow was erasing the footsteps of the one who took only 20,000 won and left 30,000 won in my pocket. I left the Wayfarer's House to go to Oran.

The Way

I think life is
the way that can't be followed
without suffering some humiliation.

If you travel
you'll find every good spot in the country
is occupied by a military post.

Hanryo waterway, the wake of the coasters crawling by on their bellies,
their passage made the way,
the foamy one.

All you who agonize over having nothing to do,
come here,
where the way changes into bubbles under you.
The anchor I dropped is my trap.

from *Mountain Sutra*

Generally speaking, every sutra concerns a journey. It's a map of nowhere.
If someone asks, say, "My father left home."
Altruism is egoism. But egoism is not altruism.
The only lesson I learned in the army is that you can make the dead look
    alive.
These days I'm locked up in my room all day. I can go anywhere.
Generally speaking, the Tao is for wandering and trading. No, the Tao is a
    form of pillaging.
Sighs fill my bladder—crabs, have you been to the heart of the sea!

Snowstorm

A few snowflakes brush the tin fish hanging from the eaves of Wonhyo
     Temple.
When I look around, the heavy snow pushes eastward, toward Kyubong
     Hermitage.

A snowstorm grants you the solitude to become your own man,
and overwhelms the snow-covered Himalayan pine forest.

Snowstorm! since there's no illumination without error,
he who reflects on his past is filled with regret.

The night snowstorm blurs the view of the Mudeung Mountains,
and I came here to be punished.

The snowstorm passes over the world
leaving a colder place—the coldest place—for me.

Now even my agony seems vulgar,
the wind passing through my body sounds brutal.

Why is sorrow poison
and hope madness?

As the snow beats my cheeks, I long for the scattered millions.
How can I know, without falling into sin,

that the road behind the mask isn't a real road,
that there's only one road before us, that some roads lead to a cliff?

In the end the night snowstorm blocks every road,
urging me to begin again from the beginning.

Lotus Flower in a Crab's Eye

I.

Wild flower seen for the first time, you deserve a name.
In what corner of my heart will you reside?
Making love to your heart, calling out your name,
I yawn again.

Unknown flower, my heart turns
too quickly to stone. I stumble on your name,
the waving flower sways even in the frozen stone.
I'm an animal susceptible to mental illness.

Waving flower, you're famous—
you met a real person,
the wind propelled by memory, in the stone.
The waving flower sways in my mind.

You exist because I called out to you.
The stone age retains the memory of fire.
When you break open the stone and remove the fire,
break my heart open and remove your name.

2.

No lotus flower in the crab's eye.
With its eyes blurred by mucus
the crab foams over the cigarette smoke,
like the froth at Pokwang.
The crab can see the lotus flower
though it can't put it in its eye.

3.

A crab in a helmet
crawls toward the sea

On its porcelain-like legs
it crosses the mud field.

It keeps coming in and out
as it spawns and dies.

There's no sea
in the heart of the sea.

The crab climbs the ladder
and rests in the Crab.

Closing The Mountain Sutra

I.

Unjoo Temple is covered with eight inches of snow
and a wooden boat is frozen with its prow pointed toward the sky.
Today I've come to shatter you to pieces
with my drop hammer.
Cancel it, cancel it!
It's time to cancel the promise.
I couldn't triumph over the world because of my innate compassion,
and the world is already so rotten.
Therefore I must abandon
my own fiction, though it still works,
before spring draws this crumbling boat
into the sky.

2.

If you pound your heart
the cloud board in the sky will keep time to the sound.
Is your sorrow that deep?
Eight inches of snow
have turned into a blanket of ice
to cover the colder sleep of the prone Buddha couple.
As if in shock
the Buddhas lie at a 15° angle.
A human hand scooped a gallon of melted snow tears
from their stone eyes.

3.

After visiting Unjoo Temple
I went to the brothel in Deain-dong on a night
when human steps had melted the snow to slush.
Though the steps covering the tracks
leave bigger tracks in their wake,
I'd like to sleep tonight with a mud body,
covering myself with a mud blanket.

"Where are you from?"

To My Wife Growing Old

Didn't I tell you
that those who love each other truly
with all their hearts and minds
never ask,
"Do you love me?"
Well, what can I say,
they just live,
they lead a life together.
They don't speak out or proclaim anything,
they just remove the sand from the other's eye
or cut the loose thread of cloth, which looks so large.

Do you remember
the late autumn fourteen years ago,
when the bleakest wind in the world blew
by the gate of your house,
at the foot of the dark village crowded with old wooden Japanese houses,
on the high embankment, with dim street lamps
and a thicket shedding leaves on the hill;
and you, returning from meeting a boy lighter than a strand of hair,
brushed the dandruff from my shoulders?
Just like that: allowing us to look at each other for a long time.
And when I got sick
you came to see me, whispering the burning words
which must have been so hard to say,
words which must have kept you up at night:
"I want to suffer through this with you."

One by one your words lifted the ethambutol and streptomycin
from the vial and turned the empty brown bottle white,
filling the empty space with your heart.
At midnight I clutched the bottle, sobbing, I knew
your love, too full and deep to use the word,
wanted us to suffer this disease together

rather than cure it—that you would lose your mind.
Then you became the reason for my life,
you replaced the future I would inhabit.

We have lived together for many years into what can safely be called an age.
As having lived means having added wrinkles to every career,
the trace of years vivid in your fingertips as you straighten my tie.
Now I must use my wet fingers not to pluck
the grey hairs scattered around your head in the morning,
but do my best to grow old with you.
Only after we have grown old together
and I can say in a feeble voice,
"Dear, we've led a good life, haven't we?"
will I be able to say,
"I love you."

Watching My Family Sleep

My wife's asleep with the TV on.
The last news, at midnight.
Nothing happened today. A HELICOPTER WITH 15 KOREAN AND AMERICAN SOL-
DIERS WENT DOWN IN THE EASTERN SEA DURING A JOINT MILITARY DRILL.
Nothing happened today. Nothing. EX-REPUBLICAN EXPRESSES DESIRE TO JOIN
THE PEOPLE'S PARTY. Nothing happened today. Nothing. A MILITARY PROSTI-
TUTE DISCOVERED IN THAILAND AFTER 40 YEARS. Nothing happened today.
Today—ONE DESERTER CAPTURED, ANOTHER KILLED—nothing happened.
Nothing happened
        today.
Although Haetae Tigers, my wife's favorite team, suffered a crushing defeat
nothing happened today.
As if nothing happened today, she's asleep with the TV on, in the TV.
Sukee Kim, a girl from a middle-class family who entrusted her money to
        the prison ten years ago.
I was afraid, first of all, that I would become bourgeois.
A fairy who descended into the wrong place. An indiscrete bourgeois.
I've drawn tattoos of poverty all over your body.
Embracing two children begotten by my desire,
you're sleeping in this world, though you seem to belong to another world.
Even when you tuck our children in and ascend to heaven, the hem of your
dress touches this world.
        What a strong bond!
She's heaving all night long at the edge of the low pressure system coming
from the Yangtze River.
        Let them be free, children are innocent.
        They've already left your womb.
If I gaze at my children sleeping at midnight
tears gather in my eyes. How can they cross the thundering sea that lies
        before them?
        Disastrous days,
        After passing through the hot and humid valley of life and death,
these innocent caterpillars will break open in this world and face the

entrance to hell.
Mother, Mother, I remember
the door of the meeting room you pushed open to go outside and cry.
That door has never closed in my mind,
all are hostages, you and my children, too.

      A deserter took hostages. His mother shouts at him through a
        megaphone.
        Mom, I'm sorry but go home!
     How can I cut this damn blood-tie?
       You devil, why did you make such a scene, why?
         Give yourself up quickly

RAISE A WHITE FLAG!   You must save your neck!
SURRENDER!   Give yourself up quickly   It's too late.
Turn yourself in quickly!   It's all over, Mom.
Mother, when you were young you cut your breast with a potsherd.
A woman who traveled to the edge of time returned,
a line of soldiers a kilometer long took turns violating her poor cunt.
The sun-eclipsed South China Sea, the tidal wave,
     please swallow
       the blindness of forty years, years without sun and moon!
The land she couldn't return to because of her shame, the land she deserted
     and forgot,
the dirty, evil land she will never forgive.
This history has no regrets, nor does it repent. Suspended days,
with no sign of repentance. The unforgiven.... Not that son of bitch again,
the molting dog? Ya, ya, it's no one's fault.
The dog visits his new owner. Ah, ah, now a dog smells my footsteps
and follows me into the castle. Now I can't enter.
My sleeping family doesn't look for me when I'm gone.
Judgment Day will come soon. Tears of remorse will drive away
the mote in my brother's eye. Brothers, believe in the world to come. A
     Muslim
youth drove a truck full of TNT and entered the next world in flames.

We too are moving toward that place, step by step, very slowly.
History is what we raise with the lever of our lives, a dull rock we strike
        with our bare hands, screaming.
Sukee, you're sleeping a dark sleep in this stone!
Are you taking a walk around your cerebrum, your next life in C-Fiber, or
        in Heaven?
The living room filled with the smell of my family seems to be a grave
in which we are all buried alive. But in the world outside this grave today
the night wind off the Yangtze River blows
and in the East Sea roiling with five-foot waves, where the bereaved
family tore out their hearts, a brightly-lit motorboat is returning
to this world, to this temporary resting place.
Sukee, someday this world will summon our children whom you embrace,
as we summoned them before.
History will contaminate these uninfected children with anger and sorrow,
        passion, and love.
Leave them alone, let them be.
        I unfold my two kids from her and fold her two arms together
        over her breasts, as if to place her in a lacquered coffin.
Either you or I will leave this world first.
If it's you, I'll bury you thousands of feet deep in my heart.

My Nude

To sit in a public bath and scrutinize every nook and corner of my body
with my own eyes is not just to scrub off the dirt
of a week or two. My whole life! What bulk I have acquired!
It's as fragile as earthenware. Broadly speaking,
what am I holding in?
Is there indeed a me? The volume of water my body spills out of the bathtub?
Only pretense constitutes me,
thirty-some years loaded with intense jealousy, a sense of inferiority,
and the vanity that likes to show off. Panting, I
have crossed the midpoint. If Taeil Chon* had lived to my age, he would
have been a saint. My life is laid bare by the lightning flash
of his short life. Ugliness, shame, humiliation. Belatedly, his
thunder roars within me now.
Thunderstruck days of my youth! I was under
the lightning rod. I was there.
Luck must have brought me there, not choice.
A silent tenant farmer within me! Perhaps he was measuring
with the visor of his Saemael hat
the field owned by the Yun family under the windbreak forest
in Bukpyung, Shinpoongri, which he never left.
Otherwise he might have crossed the Doam pass to be a potter in the next
        village.
Or would he have become a carpenter? Or a silent and careful plasterer?
Maybe his wanderlust would have led him to the city to work in construction.
He might have become a billboard painter, or a silk-threading factory guard,
or a railway worker, or drifted into the Pyoungwha market
on the Chungkye stream, bobbing in the blue veins of his cold life.
He was a firewood gatherer, a gum peddler, a newspaper boy, a secondhand
        dealer.
By the black river of poverty, behind the station, he stood for three days
and nights with an empty bowl. Bitter sewage
poured from his bowels. My hot eyes saw the red eggs of roundworms

flying in the blue sky.
I was dizzy. My father, mother, brother, sister—my whole family was
       orphaned by my dizziness.
When my older brother enlisted in the army,
I walked to Namkwangju to collect oval briquettes, counting cross-ties.
A full cargo train bound for Yeosoo passed
and the crossing gate dipped below the minimum level of living costs.
       Miserable days
before the red light.
Living in a world of chaos and woe, I emptied
out my days. Confession is disgusting.
Every self-portrait is ugly, so I've covered the stream of my life.
Many dark tributaries pass me by,
had passed by, will pass by.
Now I'm naked.
My hand touches me. This is me.

* A textile worker who immolated himself in protest.

Honam Prosthetic Shop

The strong, fleshy bodies that rush out at lunch time
to eat dog meat, wiping their sweaty faces with wet towels
as they munch on those hot Buddha natures,
look like ghosts to me,
specters who will crumble
and scatter like dust in the wind.

Body parts are on display
in the window of the Honam Prosthetic Shop
located at the corner of the rotary in front of the Chonam University
          Hospital.
The plastic limbs and arms with joints connected by bolts
and the skin-colored rubber hands which look like "real" hands;
decorated with tiny lines on their palms and blue capillaries
and even a white crescent on the pinky's fingernail,
they seem to have emerged from the ice of a previous age
and point to the Himalayan pines in front of the hospital's red brick walls
on which a gunshot's scars are still visible.
A patient with a Ringer bottle
sits under a pine tree.
Ah, only he who suffers is alive and, therefore, human.
While the blue-striped patient uniform
struggling so hard to become a real person
pushes his wheelchair up the Himalayan mountain,
the rotary in which roads from every directions converge
is jammed.
Demonstrating students must have rushed into Kumnam Street.
As if iron bones are stuck in their throats,
the iron horses break hours of poisonous gas,
while honking fart horns loudly in the traffic lanes.
As everyday life is nothing more than daily routine
and life itself depends on time

Someone rushes into the emergency room with a collapsed person on his
          back
while the Remans and Stellas* in front of the dog meat restaurant
across from the Honam Prosthetic Shop
fall to their knees like golden puppies
under the steaming sun.

* Korean passenger cars.

Landing

However high
and higher
they fly
birds
land on the earth
again.
Birds land on the earth—↓↓—and stamp their feet—KUK, KUK—
their seals of fire.
They descend
to eat, sleep, bear children, and die.
Birds disappear without leaving a trace,
and then their children, who inherited their genes,
however high
and higher
they may fly
land on the earth
again.
Never do they leave the earth!

Flower Wreath Kwangju

The violet light welds the sky to the earth.
Sakra devanam Indra glimpses the root of the sky
and hops about in ecstasy.
Under the distant cloud mat
thunder roars like drumfire.
The rain finally turns into light
and gives hope—which is futile,
because hope is a working lie.

1. MAIN ENTRANCE TO CHONAM UNIVERSITY

The gate without a door—it's finally free!
Asura hungry ghosts stand in front of the doorless gate
with their mouths gaping, displaying their hairy iron teeth
and clutching their horned iron bats.
Whoops, things usually hidden from sight are in full view.
Why are there always bad things
in front of the doors that lead to good things?
The dense blue fog of hot chili powder
crawls over the platanus forest
in the shapes of dragons and phoenixes,
and apples filled with tears
rain down on the spot.
Oh, the rascals, they go crazy.
Rascals and roughs! Passing through the door
is hardly illumination. This door is
an entrance, not an escape hatch.
They were told this in beautiful vowels and consonants,
but the hungry ghosts, who are rascals by nature,
went crazier yet, swinging their horned bats,
because they're prone to anxiety
which fear instills in them.

Then some people climbed down to Paradise Valley,
under Enlightenment Gate, picked the fire-flowers blooming everywhere,
and hurled them with a shout, "Ghosts, be gone!"
"Bigger ghosts behind them, get down!"
"Still bigger ghosts behind them, leave!"
Only the fire-flowers broke through the stratosphere
and disappeared.

The shopkeepers hosed down the street
and that night, in the very place where the flowers disappeared,
the lion constellation lit the sky.
I wonder how hot the heart must have been
before it was poured into the stone and changed into a star.

2. Public Terminal

I heard
this is the terminal from which you can travel in every direction,
where you depart and return,
return and depart.
The ox-cart which left with an overload of karma
returns to its old depot of infinite ties
with soap bubbles in its mouth,
calling to its mother in the low notes of a clarinet.
It departs and returns,
returns and departs again.
Under the wheel of the cart which has no working brakes
are worms which eat grass
and worms which eat the worms which eat grass
and fish which eat the worms which eat the worms which eat grass
and birds which eat the fish
and animals which eat the birds which eat the fish

and people which eat the animals which eat the birds which eat the fish.
Ah, the wheels,
the cause that tamps down and eats the effect!
Why did Truth take revenge
with an outrageous paradox
on the Buddha's 2524th birthday?

A boy spins the rear wheel of a bike
parked in front of the pharmacy.
The beautiful spokes of the wheel spin
like the musical gears of a clock.
Riding on a bike which has unloaded its package
the boy has already traveled through several worlds.

3. KWANGJU PARK

I heard many times in many places
that the Buddha's wreath was a sham
and that the Buddha himself should be beheaded.
Right! The Buddha's wreath was a total lie
and the Buddha was already beheaded.
One day when the tent fluttering above the wind-swept oak forest
was suddenly blacked out
men's skulls rolled like splattered watermelons.
Because people disappear
the Buddha has also disappeared,
even the Buddha himself is gone along with the people.
Their burst entrails were cooked as *sundae*,*
their bodies were removed,

* Korean sausage made of beef and bean curd stuffed in pig intestine.

only their heads are left to be steamed;
lying in the basket, they practice Zen with their eyes closed.
The bodhisattva *Avalokiteœvara,*   *Chijang* bodhisattva
The bodhisattva *Avalokiteœvara,*   *Chijang* bodhisattva
The bodhisattva *Avalokiteœvara,*   *Chijang* bodhisattva

In front of the *sundae* house, across from the oak forest plaza,
a man sears pigs' heads with a flamethrower
and his wife washes away the blood of the slimy entrails
in a large rubber basin.
The blood flows into Kwangju Stream,
into the dark blue sky, into the distant Southern River,
and finally into Paradise River.
One day
from the sand dunes of Paradise River
a stone Buddha without a neck
floated by,
unearthed by a flood.
A delegation of National Assembly members from the Kwangju Democratic
        Uprising
made a special visit to examine them.
But the Buddha always exists
like this—
a being who has disappeared,
neither dead
nor resurrected yet.

4. KWANGCHON-DONG

It's just as I heard.
Spring of Light, a name older than Kwangju.
Sometimes the professional baseball broadcast shows

the shy, beautiful rays of twilight
half-hidden by cirrus feathers
in the sky above the leftfield bleachers in Mudeung Stadium.
When it grows dark,
when all the lights have gone out in Kwangju,
girls change shifts at the main entrance to Ilsan Textile Factory
and Sangwon Yun's sister looks for the cut thread
under the florescent light.

"Brother, are you still there at the end of this thread?
You taught me with a dim light
that the world is made entirely by man.
But now, under the quivering florescent light,
you still haven't escaped this world,
you're stuck somewhere in this skein of thread
which is long enough to circle the world."
The light thread which the laborer bodhisattva sewed
under the florescent light
is unraveling in the seams of the clothes
of the people walking along the Chungjangro at night.

5. SILK RIVER RUNNING ENDLESSLY NORTH

A taxi arrives at Keumnamro via Kwangchon-dong
and rushes through the torrential rain, spreading wings of water on both
        sides.
The water's so clear
that black apartment buildings can be seen through it.
I'd like to ask
if there's a road below the river.
It seems it was only a few months ago that the road
sank from sight and become a relic.

The river, strafed,
is a river of ink which breaks out in rashes.
I heard
that if a black cow walks into the river then out
she'll become as white as velvet,
but I wonder how she can walk into a river deep as silk,
a river that looks deep but doesn't even cover your ankle once you're in.
The driver says he went there briefly
on the back of an elephant;
hence his hair has already turned white.
The gingkoes along the street rise above the water
and never bend even in high winds and torrential rains,
instead, they raise their voices against them.
I get out of the taxi at the Y building by the provincial office
and see how I have traveled,
and the Silk River running endlessly north
flows into the sky of the opaque, invisible Blue Sky River.

6. PROVINCIAL OFFICE

The time for the appointment has come and gone
but no one has appeared.
Tired of waiting, the lion rises from his seat,
shakes his body, and roars loudly. A drumming roar
that tears open the sky in the shape of lightning.
Hail begins to fall,
flowers turn into stars turn into stones.
No one is likely to arrive in this hailstorm
but Truth occasionally breaks an appointment and appears.
As what we long for comes
unawares while we wait
for the hail to end,

for the storm to end,
the glass boughs will soar above the trees
from the fountain in front of the provincial office.
As if someone had sucked stifled tears with all his might
and sprayed the drops over the glass trees,
Mani* gem flowers will bloom
on transparent boughs and turn into lights.
Then bells will ring in all the temples, churches,
cathedrals, and shrines,
and the sound of temple bells will follow
the lights of the lotus-shaped paper lanterns everyone carries.
Leaving stores, banks, and warehouses wide open,
the people, like a river spreading its joyful heart,
will spontaneously put on luminous faces;
the young will ride on their shoulders and the old will carry each other on
          their backs,
with the children in front,
decorated with flowers, horsehair hats, and shining shoes,
from every direction, they will all flow into
Keumnamro, the labor office, and the provincial office
like a roaring river.
Then Mudeung Mountain, which flowed out of Sumi Mountain
and laid still, finally unfurls its wings
and soars above, shattering
the radar base on its pate.
Shouts for joy on earth,
thunder music, mysterious fireworks in the sky.
At the corner of the road to Mangwol
billions of bo tree flowers gaze at the world with joy,
whispering to one other.
At the Keyrim a golden-feathered cock cries,
soaring above the forest in a cloud…
Then thieves, hooligans, rapists,

national security lawbreakers, and aging communists
walk out of prison, bursting into laugher.
That night, when the lotus moon floats brightly
over Moon Mountain, over the slopes
touched by the Thousand Rivers, a dog that traveled in many worlds
and saw the lotus moon in the water for the first time
returns to the mountain, howling like a wolf.

* Precious beads said to end unhappiness and catastrophes and purify water

Part III

Sitting Cross-legged and Thinking about the World Outside

A black longicorn beetle under the sun—
blindness is a sacred disease!

A flatfish lying on the bottom of the tank
looks outside at a bike passing, carrying goods. Can it see?

What can it do? It's already too late,
it understands the situation.

It sees the world outside—unlimited, impassable space.
The day wanes. A black ox weeps in the doorway.

I'd Like to Stay Here Longer

Pop! On the day the cherry pops
its white popcorn blossoms all over the sky
you should get away from this world
and vacation in its shade.

If you close your eyes,
a sound-tree
filled not with blossoms
but buzzing bees
about to fly off,
flashes in this world.

If you open your eyes, a young family
pushes a baby stroller under the blossoming cherry;
when they pass with the shade of the blossoms on their white blouses
laughter breaks over this popcorn world.

They are no longer of this world.
The cherry road on my way to Naejang Temple: on a day like this,
when another world is glimpsed,
let's stay here a little longer.

Holy May

At Manwol cemetery
I smell a kind of breath on the mountain,
like my daughter's breath after she brushes her teeth,
welcoming us with a bag of acacia blossoms.
It should not only be on your deathbed
that the sacred suddenly wraps you in its arms;
the sunlight showering through the leaves
makes my face blush.
With a mouthful of blossoms that taste like mint toothpaste,
I gaze at the cemetery from afar;
the respect you gain after death is like static electricity
generated by the accident, transience, and meaninglessness of your life.
When you were alive, your life was no better than a worm's,
but the people who like to hand out their name cards
circle your tomb, a huge bubble.
Holy May: acacia blossoms shake their white handkerchiefs
which suddenly make me sneeze.

August 16

On the veranda, in my hanging garden—
morning glories come from God knows where.
Did my good neighbor tie them to the pulley
and send the stars upwards?
When I hear the unexpected chirring of cicadas in the apartment complex
or feel a sudden chill in the midsummer morning,
my skin grows sad
and I shudder in fear.
The Peruvian summer must be passing in Peru.
When I feel time ebb from my body,
I break out in goose flesh
as if I had been poisoned by lacquer.
Gazing for a long time at a pubic hair
on the blanket, I lick my finger
and pick it up.
I wonder when I will acknowledge my life,
like my good neighbor
who ties stars with "the thread of the whole world"
and delivers them as a gift to someone.

Cherry Blossoms Under the Mercury Lamp

When the cherry blossoms opened
on the Sazik Park slope,
I used to get sick
and drunk
just to endure.
When the blossoms breaking into this world from that world
shone under the mercury lamp,
any evil seemed permissible under that tree.
It was a spring night, and I wanted to hug and kiss someone
or cut someone with a broken *Soju* bottle.

When all the blossoms grew ugly and fell to the ground,
like my adolescent wish to die over the guilt
I felt right after masturbating,
and like my sins dropping into the heap of dung,
I already knew
my life would turn out like this.

But now I envy
the light of murderous intent and the sin.
On my way home after seeing off
my love (I asked her to leave),
I pray for a blessing
and then look up to see
the mercury lamps among the cherry blossoms
illuminating this life of mine.

The Meal of This World

Although Mother survived a crisis and is home from the hospital
she's not the same—her mind is hazy.
How can I express my sorrow
when she insists that our guests in black suits
are detectives from the KCIA or another branch of intelligence come to
      arrest my brother,
or when she strikes matches in the living room to start a fire in the kitchen?
Now she even forgets to call to God,
the very God
before whom she knelt at dawn and prayed on the cold floor of the church
when I was imprisoned and suffered a little
and my brother was chased day and night by the police.
To end this blackout of her soul
I was ready to convert again,
calling to the head of the shrine I escaped from.
So I took her to the Hallelujah prayer house,
where she broke my heart with her blank expression.
A few days ago, when she collected her mind,
she gave my wife her cross-shaped golden necklace
saying, "All this is utterly useless."
Whether she was bequeathing gold or a cross,
I felt that she was cleaning out her life
and got angry at her for no reason.
I shuddered at her disposing even of her cross.
Mother, how can you cross the river alone without this?
After visiting Chonju Jesus Hospital, I prepared her favorite meal
of fish but she didn't eat much.
A meal with an old sick mother is like a meal prepared for a memorial service.
Though I cleaned the fish and placed it on her rice
she only said, "help yourself while you have an appetite."
Something besides a fish bone was stuck in my throat
and I snuck into the living room.
The Verona World Cup ball was bouncing wildly on the TV screen.

Wellbeing (I)

When I get up in the morning, first I open the door to my mother's room.
When I was a boy, opening my eyes,
I would put my ears to my mother's nose, and feel relieved.
Every morning I carefully open the door to see whether she is dead or not.
How desperate is love
on the threshold of this tiny door?
Hiding her dung-smeared clothes in the closet,
she's ashamed of her life
which hasn't left her yet.
When I use the hose in the shower to wash her private parts,
through which she pushed me into this world,
and brush her mussed-up hair,
she's a tiny girl sitting nicely on the mattress,
sneezing.
Let's not talk about lightness, please.

Sacred Meal

When an old man eats alone,
something starts inside him;
when he picks up the *ramen*,*
covering the noodle house menu with his bulky body,
a memory of fighting with his younger brother over cold steamed rice
suddenly revives to choke him.

The sacredness of eating,
of serving the body a spoonful of the world,
the hot life clinging to the cold rice of this world!
Look at the disheveled hair of the man
who eats his meal alone!
I wonder why it brings tears to my eyes to see the gaping mouth
of an old man eating a spoonful of steamed rice served in soup
at a *sundae* house behind Pagoda Park.

* Korean instant noodles

My Pond, My Sanitarium

When I remove my clothes in the bathroom,
there's something else I'd like to remove.
I feel within myself
an old crepe myrtle dreaming of transmigration,
of changing its body into another life.

Like bent bodies entering the tub
curved crepe myrtles,
three hundred years old,
stand along the edge of the pond.

When the red flowers of August glow
like charcoal exposed to the wind,
growing brighter near me,
I'd like to plunge naked into that tub of flowers
and emerge with a new life.
Wearing the petals like sparks of fire on my head,
I'll laugh. If friends visit from Seoul,
I'll tell them it's a bruised man who dresses
the world, and when they leave
I'll call them back
to lay these flowers of strong medicine
on their eyes.

St. Charlie Chaplin

In the last scene of *Modern Times*, our "innocent victim,"
Charlie Chaplin, ties his shoes beside the street and,
smiling in his own sad way, says to his love,
"But don't say you'll die."
At which you wept again, lacking a strong will.

It might be my beggar disposition,
but I've hungered for you to say,
"How do you survive now?"
Saints used to say these words to beggars.
You have to live, don't you?
Therefore please survive by any means.

I'll Sit in a Cloudy Tavern Some Day

My daughter just got her first period. I can't hug her anymore.
Grim is my life.
I can no longer peek into her diary.
On the photos of starving Africans in which only their eyes shine,
under a poster proclaiming, "Let's share the bread of love," she recorded
the amount of our donation. Leaving her room, I
walk around outside—outside;
I wonder when I fell into the habit of avoiding people
because of my suspicion that someone is always watching me.
Like the clothes falling from the hanger,
my life would crumble into its present position;
I can't endure my awkwardness lodged in its fat leather sack.
Well, is there anything more vulgar than sorrow?

Therefore I'll sit in a cloudy tavern some day,
in a leather sack grown comfortable with age,
and listening calmly to the noisy chatter behind my back,
I'll gaze with regret at the wine left in my glass.

But the problem is whether I can accept
being such a beautiful "useless man."

Midwinter Picture Seen Through Glass

New Year's Day, empty apartment—
a magpie draws U's
under the snowy boughs of Umon Mountain.
The balcony window frames and mounts
a midwinter landscape, about 8' x 12'.
Soon a feather drops into the frame.
Should I place a cup of green tea in that cold house?

The Forest of Bronze Marronniers

I.

I came to Dongsung-dong, like a man
who in the end returns to his former wife. I took out a cigar
and put it back—after hesitating under the marronnier
in which the odor of sour wine lingered from my first kiss,
while someone played guitar in the hallway of the psychology lab.
Who was dragged into prison and the army, and who entered the temple?
Though youth is what drives everyone to wake at midnight in lament,
Professor Y, who taught Greek history, was looking beyond the clock tower
at the cloudy sky on October 17, 1972—the date cast in iron
on which the soldiers set their sights on the empty campus of the bronze
            forest.
Since that day, the reason sleeping in the ivory tower
seems to have left me adrift on perilous waters.
That's why I couldn't go mad
or become a transcendent sage; nowadays,
when nothing can be expected from mankind,
I still believe it's the last resort for us
because I can hardly find it in me.
Lullulullu lullulu, I whistled an old song like the sour wine
and passed the bronze forest: warm breaths of my first kiss in the copper
            boughs.
Like the handsome youth who descends with golden boughs in his hand,
I sauntered about the marronnier,
with the sleeves of my blue shirts rolled, wearing the sky of poetry on my
            head.
That sour kiss opened the knob of my love,
but is life just an endless repetition of chaos and turmoil?
Where I used to play poker, junior high school girls wearing makeup
were break dancing, and palm readers sat
on the steps of the library Prof. Y tried to climb.
A black dog leashed to a dead tree glared down at me.

My old lover, who left me to move to Germany, entered Samteo Gallery
with her daughter holding a balloon. Seized with fear,
I cut the pregnant tree with a stone knife. Behind the tree
L, a congressman now, whispered to me, then quickly disappeared.
When I heard that YS had proclaimed martial law again and I should go
into hiding, I don't know why but I was happy.
The black dog ran away, jumping over the forest.

2.

The next day when I went to pick up my car, which in my drunkenness I
          had left
in front of the theatre, the roof of my Pride was covered with leaves,
golden stickers someone had torn off the bronze forest and pasted there.
A tree can offer cozy lodgings to the one who violates the day!

Prayer for a Pine Tree

Taking a walk up the hill behind campus,
I forgave the man under the pine tree
covered with snow as if in penance
and came down. Though it isn't leaving you
to keep my dignity,
but accepting you as you are
that bends me like this.
The pine tree, the most elegant tree
in the world,
which never loses its austere bearing,
shivers for a while
and brushes the snow off its head.

A Herd of Black Goats Goes to Joge Temple

When the bereaved family left for Guam,
the island set afloat on the sea by the wind,
fish bones like the teeth of a comb
became fossils on a white plate.
Anyone can go that way.
Some ride on a bus whose driver is unconscious.
At the Jongno 2 ga where a left turn is prohibited
a herd of black goats goes to Joge Temple
to report on the tragedy.
Then CNN broadcasts the Taeguk*
of the broken-tail assembly.

Felled trees on the high slopes of the island.
Whenever their limbs are twisted
they swell the muscles of the wind
to support the hanging god
like dwarf weight lifters.

* The Great Absolute in Chinese philosophy; the circle with the figures for Yin and Yang; the symbol of Korean Airlines.

Diary of the Fat Sofa

I got up early in the morning, brushed my teeth, washed my face, and sat at
    the table.
(Not true. To be honest, when I got up late this morning and sat at the table,
my wife asked me to brush my teeth and wash my face before coming to the
    table.
So I brushed my teeth, washed up, and sat at the table.)
Because there was a bowl of reheated soup before me
I yawned long and hard even though it was morning,
like an animal in the zoo opening its lower jaw
without a noise, closing its ugly eyes.

Thus began another day for me.
A boring meal, but once I started to eat I ate more.
That animal might have experienced the same thing: the recollection of life
is all that keeps me alive now.
I'm so comfortable I'm miserable. I got up in the morning, brushed my teeth,
washed my face, sat at the table, ate breakfast,
rinsed out my mouth (my wife loathes the sound of me rinsing out the bits
of food stuck between my teeth when I move my cheeks as if to gargle.
She warned me that I was getting gross.)
I sat down on the sofa.
But, sofa!
That word reminds me of "soap" or "soft"
for no reason, and a "bubble chair."
This chair-like sofa, which looks like a fertile woman from the Paleolithic Age
with huge breasts, is in fact covered with imitation leather.
Murmuring to myself, "Oh, sofa, my Mommy" with an English accent,
and shrugging my shoulders like a Yankee,
I sat down on the sofa.

This morning, I got up, washed my face, ate breakfast, and sat down on the sofa.
From the sofa, the living room looks like a stage for a foreign drama:
an imitation leather sofa in the center, the clock on the wall showing 9 A.M.,

in the back a still life drawn after Cézanne, a TV set,
a dragon tree near the window, the awkward book shelf
on which lie three clothbound volumes of Marx's *Capital* (Moscow: Progress
Press), the books I brought in to display but never read, and the aquarium
bubbling continuously.
But there is no tragedy worth translating on this stage.
Only a man got up, washed, ate, and sat down on the sofa in the morning:
a man who has grown so fat you can't identify him from old photos,
a man who will not lift a finger,
whose wife now says even his mouth smells bad.
When this man sits vacantly on the sofa and yawns, like the animal in the zoo,
and blinks away tears from his eyes,
and his wife appears stage left (from the kitchen) to sit beside him
stroking his chin and telling him to shave,
he hugs her and calls her "Mommy."

When his wife, who with better luck might have become a pianist, comes
          to him
and strokes me before she leaves to give a piano lesson, I feel good.
When my wife gives a haircut to the man on the sofa
and sneaks up on him during his nap to trim my toenails,
or when she lays his head on her knee to clean my ears, I'm happy.
When she brings him green vegetable juice in the morning and then wipes
          his mouth,
I watch her with a smile.
I wish she would help him get up and bathe him,
and serve me food and clean up my shit.
I'd like to entrust the rest of his life to her.
I'd like to be a human vegetable who breathes only through his nose
and lies still, blinking earnest eyes, and then she divines his thought
          and does it for him.
The dragon tree needs sunshine every now and then,
          and so she has to raise the blinds,

she can sympathize with it but can't take responsibility for it. I don't want
to leave this hospital room.

I got up, washed my face, ate, and sat on the sofa,
and stayed home alone all day long, because my wife went out.
Sinking into the sofa, which resembles an old fat Stone Age mother,
I listened in silence to the clock on the wall gnawing at what remains of my life.
Though too much of my spare time has dropped like the dung of silk worms,
I accept this too as life. I won't meddle with it.
Nothing is harder to endure than the spectacle of a man becoming
        a comic figure;
wu-wei will thus be my style for enduring the rest of my life.
It's also a pity when a man becomes a cartoon figure;
however humiliating it is to acknowledge
he has lived in vain into his forties,
the only way to redeem such a life is
to accept the fact that I am nothing.
It's a little hard to accept this,
but isn't an idler better than the malice
of the people who plot revenge against the world, however meager that may be!
I enjoyed myself in style all day long on the sofa.
Even as the lamenting clock spreads its long and short hands
and makes the afternoon as splendid as a peacock standing in the light,
and the silk worms who nibbled at innocent time (I didn't lift a hand)
prepare another round of life,
and two Sumatras, like the fossils of tropical fish, lined up to thrust themselves
into my face as I gazed vacantly into the aquarium,
I feel the aerorium in which I was placed.
I yawn again like the fish
and the MBC News Desk is showing the former naval chief in black Ray Bans
posing for photographers in front of the Public Prosecutors Office.

Shouting "Oh my sofa, oh my Mommy," I sprang from the sofa
when my wife returned. (She appeared stage right,
holding a plastic bag of food from the grocery store.)
Today I ate dinner, watched TV, and slept.
Before I went to sleep, I brushed my teeth because my wife asked me to.
I must mention that my wife smiled sadly at me
when I posed in front of the bathroom like the former naval chief.
Oh, yeah, it was mostly sunny; the high in Seoul and the central area was 28°C.
When I open the door to the master bedroom, the stage lights switch off.
A man shouts in the darkness: "Can you hear the sound of the wind
blowing across the corn field?" The river below the fifteen-story building,
I didn't know until now that the river shines at night like a long plastic strip.
Miserable aerorium dwellers, goodbye, bye-bye!

Afterward

Beyond the Borders of Inside and Outside: Zen Romanticism and the Poetics of Hybridity

Professor Chan Je Wu
Sogang University, Seoul, Korea

1. A Tragic View of the World and Aesthetic Depth

Ji-woo Hwang is the representative Korean poet of the past twenty years. He has a unique sense of language, an intuitive grasp of reality, an experimental imagination. From the ordinary, trivial, and vulgar he draws extraordinary perceptions. His unfamiliar sensibility shocks readers into new perceptions. He transforms the non-poetic experiences of daily life into poetry.

For a long time, he couldn't reconcile himself to the world, unable to find a meaningful semantic identity between his self and the world. So he had to fight the world or overcome his divided self. And this conflict is the wellspring of his poetic energy.

He was born in 1952, during the Korean War, in the port town Haenam, on the South Sea, just seven years after Korea had been freed from the Japanese colonial yoke. He grew up in a poor family, and went to college in the early 1970s, during the military dictatorship. He studied philosophy and aesthetics in college and graduate school, during which he was arrested and tortured for his anti-government activities. He began to publish his poems in 1980 and has since written seven books of poetry. For his work Hwang has received many of Korea's most prestigious literary awards, among them, the Sooyoung Kim Literary Award, the Hyundae Literary Award, the Sowol Poetry Award, and the Daesan Literary Award. And his versatile artistic talents are on display in his work as a dramatist, a sculptor, and an art critic.

The violence of the war, economic difficulty, and political tyranny must have forced Hwang to "suffer a certain disgrace," for no poet can be free from the suffering of his people. In this respect his family makeup is interesting: his elder brother is a Zen monk, his younger brother is a labor union leader, his mother is a Christian. "The Meal of This World" seems to stem from the poet's own experience. And the sorrow of his mother who "knelt at dawn and prayed on the cold floor of the church / when I was imprisoned and suffered a little/ and my brother was chased day and night by the police" is not just the sorrow of his own family but of the entire nation.

Though his complaints sometimes sound too much like Baudelaire, Hwang does suffer the agony of existence. In a phrase "Both sides of the supermarket wall are covered with mirrors. One mirror watches another mirror, and the mirror watches the mirror that watches the mirror…" the poet describes the mechanism of surveillance and punishment, but the readers see the poet's eyes observing the depths of the mirror, i.e, *mis-en-abime.*

Certainly the poet's eye has changed with his circumstances. But the political imagination still underlies his poetry, as we can see in "The Forest of Bronze Marronniers" and "My Nude." Nevertheless his political imagination radically differs from unfiltered, graphic descriptions of reality. For him, the political is transformed into the poetical. His unique imagination not only sublimates mundane political events into a philosophical discourse but also draws aesthetic issue from the secular landscape.

2. Dialectics of Negation and Zen Romanticism

"I go out / as usual, the strangest person in the fifth republic," Hwang writes. Indeed he was an alienated stroller in the 1980s, when the symptoms of industrial capitalism and political tyranny were most pronounced. If

Baudelaire portrayed his melancholy and anxiety as nightmares, Hwang reads "everything in the streets"—that which has occurred and that which has not. Through his dialectics of negation, his early work succeeds in drawing poetic life from dire reality. Though he diagnoses the sickness of reality, he doesn't succumb to sentimental moaning, but rather presents concrete reality strange through his sharp wit and parody, as in the title poem of his first book, *Even Birds Leave the World* (1983):

> Before the movie starts
> we stand up and listen to the national anthem.
> Forming groups on Eulsuk Island,
> on three thousand miles of beautiful land,
> the flocks of white birds,
> honking and giggling among themselves,
> take flight from a field of reeds.
> They separate this world from theirs
> and fly away to some place beyond this world
> in single, double, and triple file.
> I wish we could giggle among ourselves, and behave outrageously,
> and form our own lines to file out in.
> We'd like to separate our world from this world
> and carry it on our backs
> and fly away to some place beyond this world.
> But when we hear "Keep the Korean people safe forever!"
> we all collapse
> into our chairs.

In the 1980s everyone in the theater had to stand for the national anthem before the movie could start, while clips showing the beauty of the Korean peninsular played on the screen. Hwang captures this orderly scene juxtaposed to the birds that "separate their world from this world / and fly away to some place beyond this world"—a conspicuous image of escape. Though we too would like to fly away, we can only collapse into our seats.

Why was he so desperate to escape? So that he could live. In a land in which people are nothing more than hostages sleeping "a dark stony sleep,"

Hwang does not say that reality must be negated. Instead he presents it in an unfamiliar way, dramatizing the conflict between his own existence and reality. And if his poems provide details of an oppressive reality, they are far from dry realism. He is, by nature, a poet of a romantic disposition. An early work, "Like Dew on the Grass," shows his intuitive side. He discerns movement in dew, which is customarily regarded as a symbol for evanescence. He finds an image of fire in the dew and juxtaposes the contrasting images to open up a new horizon. His poetry thus transcends and reconciles the contraries such as "being" and "non-being,"

After his second book of poetry, *From Winter Tree to Spring Tree* (1985), Hwang dove under the surface of the ordinary to find new meaning. In a long painful journey, he searched for "the morning country" over which he could fly like a bird—a place where life might be renewed. But is there such a place? Its sheer impossibility made it the object of his desire. Therefore we should "stay here a little longer" to glimpse another world—a yearning he questions and deconstructs until he discovers a multi-layered perception of the limitless universe.

What can Hwang do in such a complex universe? He might have resigned himself to fate. But the poet adamantly struggled to find a liberating space beyond his incapacitating despair. Zen provided him energy with which to transcend the borders of the inside and the outside. A Zen master famously said, "I cannot find the footsteps one has left behind"—a sentiment echoed in lines like "But the crab can see the lotus flower / which it can't put into its eye" or "There's no sea / in the heart of the sea." But Hwang's Zen Romanticism is different from a naïve negation of or escape from reality. He acknowledges the harsh reality of existence and transcends it by crawling sideways, like a crab. A concrete and dreamy free will reaching for "the world outside—unlimited, impassable space"—this is the core of Hwang's Zen Romanticism.

3. Bodily Imagination and the Poetics of Hybridity

Ji-woo Hwang's poetic discourse derives from the concrete particulars of reality, especially in his images of corporeality. Interest in the body has been a worldwide trend since Nietzsche, but Hwang's inquiry has special meaning because the bodies he depicts belong to people whose "minds are dead but whose bodies are still alive." In most cases, the bodies in Hwang's poems are wounded from the depths of their inner souls. They are, if you like, similar to the winter trees described in one of his most acclaimed poems, "From Winter Tree to Spring Tree":

> A tree becomes a tree
> from its own body.
> With its whole body a tree becomes a tree.
> Sinking its whole naked trunk into the earth
> at -13°C and -20°C
> and raising its head,
> the tree stands naked and helpless.
> Raising its two hands, as if to be punished,
> the tree lifts its body and long suffering life.
> "It can't be like this." "It shouldn't be like this."
> Though its whole body burns with anger and frustration
> the tree resists and endures, and then pushes its body
> from below zero to above zero, to 5° and 13°C,
> the tree pushes itself so blindly
> its whole body is bruised
> and crushed.
> While its body is broken apart
> it pushes out new sprouts with its hot tongue
> which will grow green leaves slowly, gradually, suddenly.
> Striking its body into April's blue skies
> the tree becomes a tree from its whole body.
> Ah, at last,
> the blossoming tree is a blossoming tree
> from nothing but its own body.

The winter tree becomes a blossoming spring tree from its own body—a natural process, which the poet regards as the body's will. Here it is impossible to distinguish the body from the heart. They exist beyond such demarcation.

Hwang has a tragic vision, so most of his "bodies" are as naked as trees in winter. They resemble the poet's life "crumbl[ing] into its present position." And because Hwang can look at the inside within the inside and the outside within the outside, he also watches the body within and without the body. "When I take off my clothes in the bathroom," he writes, "there's something else I'd like to remove"—his old life.

His desire for a new life leads him to unfurl his imagination and experiment with form. He destroys poetic grammar, employs unconventional language, incorporates newspaper ads, articles, cartoons, and graffiti. He deconstructs received forms, customs, and authority, creating a new poetics of open form. His poetry thus deviated from the pure lineage of lyrical poetry. His impure poetry destroys the traditional body of poetry and creates a new body from the multifarious bodies of reality. This heterogeneous deconstruction and reconstruction is at once a physical and a chemical process. This trend is conspicuous in his mingling of traditional genres such as lyric, epic, and drama. Many of his poems contain elements of narrative and drama. And it should be noted that he is not only a successful dramatist who has written famous plays including *May Jesus*, but also a professor of drama at the Korean Academy of Theater.

Hwang creates his own hybrid poetics, employing various styles and genres. This new style might be called "dramatic narrative lyric." "Diary of the Fat Sofa," which enjoyed a long dramatic run in Korea, best represents his poetics of hybridity, reinterpreting the modern theme of ennui through *wu-wei*, the traditional norm of life in the Orient. Laotze's *wu-wei* gains new meaning for Hwang's aeroreum dwellers:

> I got up, washed my face, ate, and sat on the sofa,
> and stayed home alone all day long, because my wife went out.
> Sinking into the sofa, which resembles an old fat Stone Age mother,
> I listened in silence to the clock on the wall gnawing at what remains
>   of my life.
> Though too much of my spare time has dropped like the dung of silk
>   worms,
> I accept this too as life. I won't meddle with it.
> Nothing is harder to endure than the spectacle of a man becoming a

comic figure;
wuwei will thus be my style for enduring the rest of my life.
It's also a pity when a man becomes a cartoon figure;
however humiliating it is to acknowledge
he has lived in vain into his forties,
the only way to redeem such a life is
to accept the fact that I am nothing.
It's a little hard to accept this,
but isn't an idler better than the malice
of the people who plot revenge against the world, however meager that
    may be!
I enjoyed myself in style all day long on the sofa.

In this dramatic narrative lyric written in the form of a diary, Hwang captures daily routines in vivid terms. The loafer tries to endure his meaningless life through wu-wei, rather than by wallowing in malice. Accepting that he is nothing, does nothing, he paradoxically leaves nothing undone. This is a new horizon of life he dreams of reaching. We can glimpse an aspect of post-capitalist ontology, a form of emancipation in which one exists like the air.

Hwang's poetics of hybridity achieve not only dynamic form but also thematic depth. Though his poetry stretched too far the traditional norms of poetry, his experiment blessed modern poetry with new possibilities; his poetry not only shows how to incorporate the spirit of the times, which cannot find expression in short lyrics, but also affords a channel for reveries. This reverie is in keeping with Hwang's vision of overcoming Descartean dichotomy and logocentricism. His effort to leap the borders of inside and outside, to excavate new meaning on the border, is part of his poetic strategy. Though he sometimes laments that "When the life and culture of an age turn pornographic, I wonder what's the use of writing poems, lying on the cold floor at dawn. What a funny thing to do," Hwang never ceases to dream of an aesthetic vision with which to overcome realty. Because he writes poems with his aching body, his poetic reverie cannot but be dangerous and painful. Hwang's own words, from an essay titled "Time for Literature to Retire," best summarize his poetic intentions:

In the 1990s my poetic strategy was to probe events occurring in my heart. I experimented with pseudo-madness—depression, deprivation, schizophrenia, hallucination, panic, flights of ideas—and thought this was a way to fight the hellish chaos of daily life. To call this black humor risks disaster. Simulating sickness can develop into real sickness, and my faked illness often left me dizzy. Though every hallucination is not poetic, certain hallucinations have poetic elements. I had a similar experience with Zen; though every Zen experience was not poetic, some struck me as poetic. Such an exploration for poetry required me to dive into the depths of my literary map. My indulgence in psychic abnormalities was a kind of "dark Zen." I suffered illness like a patient, which reminded me of Vimalakrti, who discovered his vision through his sickened body.

About the Poet

Ji-woo Hwang was born in 1952, during the Korean War, in the southern port town Haenam, and studied aesthetics and philosophy at college in the early 1970s, during which he was arrested and tortured for his anti-government activities. He began to publish his poems in 1980 and has since written seven books of poetry including *Even Birds Leave the World* (1983), *From Winter Tree to Spring Tree* (1985), and *I'll Sit in a Cloudy Tavern Some Day* (1990). For his work, Hwang has received many of Korea's most prestigious literary awards, among them the Sooyoung Kim Literary Award, the Hyundae Literary Award, the Sowol Poetry Award, and the Daesan Literary Award. He teaches Drama at the Korean Academy of Theater.

About the Translators

Won-Chung Kim is a professor of English Literature at Sungkyunkwan University in Seoul, Korea, where he teaches contemporary American poetry, ecological literature, and translation. He earned his Ph.D. in English at the University of Iowa in 1993. He has translated Chiha Kim's *Heart's Agony* and Choi Seungho's *Flowers in the Toilet Bowl*. He will soon publish translations of Hyonjong Chong's *Trees of the World* and an anthology of Korean ecological poets. He has also translated E.T. Seton's *The Gospel of the Redman* and Bernd Heinrich's *In a Patch of Fireweed* into Korean.

Christopher Merrill has published four collections of poetry, including *Watch Fire*, for which he received the Peter I. B. Lavan Younger Poets Award from the Academy of American Poets; several edited volumes, among them, *The Forgotten Language: Contemporary Poets and Nature*; and four books of nonfiction, *The Grass of Another Country: A Journey Through the World of Soccer*, *The Old Bridge: The Third Balkan War and the Age of the Refugee*, *Only the Nails Remain: Scenes from the Balkan Wars*, and *Things of the Hidden God: Journey to the Holy Mountain*. He directs the International Writing Program at The University of Iowa.

The Korean Voices Series